THE SECRETS OF PEACEMAKING

BOOKS BY GREG STONE

Taming the Wolf: Peace through Faith

Preparing for Mediation: A Practical Guide

THE SECRETS OF PEACEMAKING

Greg Stone

Taming the Wolf Institute, Westlake Village 91361

Copyright © 2019 by Taming the Wolf Institute

All rights reserved. For permissions, contact tamingthewolf.com.

Taming the Wolf Institute is a 501(c)3 that delivers peacemaking instruction and services.

Excerpt(s) from *Jesus of Nazareth: The Infancy Narratives* by Pope Benedict XVI, translation copyright © 2012 by Libreria Editrice Vaticana. Used by permission of Image Books, an imprint of Random House, a division of Penguin Random House LLC. All rights reserved.

Excerpt(s) from *Jesus of Nazareth: From the Baptism in the Jordan to the Transfiguration* by Pope Benedict XVI, copyright © 2007 by Libreria Editrice Vaticana, Citta del Vaticano. Copyright © 2007 by RCS Libri S.p.A., Milan. Used by permission of Doubleday Religion, an imprint of Random House, a division of Penguin Random House LLC. All rights reserved.

ISBN: 978-0-9848853-2-9

Cover art by Tracy Stone

Book design by Tracy Stone and Lindsay Stone

Printed in the United States of America

To the memory of my pastor and friend,
Rev. Jarlath Dolan

CONTENTS

PROLOGUE

The Great Hunger   xvii

INTRODUCTION

The Peace of Christ Revealed   1

ONE

Theology, Reason, Idealism   5
   Reflection   15

TWO

Personal Philosophies   17
   Reflection   21

THREE

Culture & Love   23
Reflection   27

FOUR

Healing Human & Divine Relationships   29
Reflection   31

FIVE

Aligning Disordered Will   33
Reflection   37

SIX

Transforming False Self   39
Reflection   45

SEVEN

Evil & The Spiritual Warrior   47
Reflection   55

EIGHT

Mystical Union & Spiritual Healing   57
Reflection   61

NINE

Peace in the End Times   63
Reflection   67

TEN

And the Rest... 69
  Reflection 73

APPENDIX

Core Principles 75

NOTES 81

...we could not love if we were not first loved by God. God's grace always precedes us, embraces us and carries us. But it also remains true that man is called to love in return, he does not remain an unwilling tool of God's omnipotence: he can love in return or he can refuse God's love.

Pope Benedict XVI[1]

PROLOGUE

THE GREAT HUNGER

Humanity hungers for peace. Men and women call out to God, asking him to soften hearts. People pray that peace will descend upon the world like dewfall. Amidst worldly struggle, souls long for tranquility.

All too often, serenity is found only in our dreams. Turmoil and conflict are life's constant companions. In this fallen world, cries of human suffering clash with sweet promises of heavenly peace. Mankind shares the disappointment of failing to secure lasting world peace. Tranquility seems to be a distant dream.

Yet, while we must acknowledge the harshness of the present reality, we must not lose hope. We must not cease our efforts to hasten peace. In spite of all invitations to despair, we must continue to soften hearts, one by one.

We cannot afford to retreat to the sidelines. We cannot simply pray for our arrival in the next world where peace reigns. That is not an option. Instead, we must actively work to hasten the arrival of the peace that Christ promised. We are called to the vocation of peacemaking and we must respond.

The Secrets of Peacemaking was written to shine light on the path to peace and thus assist peacemakers in their sacred quest. It was meant to guide aspiring peacemakers to the path that leads to the Peace of Christ.

INTRODUCTION

THE PEACE OF CHRIST REVEALED

Today, the secrets of peacemaking remain hidden in plain sight—ever present yet buried under mounds of confusion regarding man's true nature. Throughout history, this lack of clarity has obfuscated the path to peace.

Bewildered by the complexity of the subject, many give up the study of peacemaking; others become lost in a fog of abstractions. Misdirection sends people looking for peace in the wrong directions. Many peace studies programs, tainted by secular views, build their curricula on flawed foundations, which in turn produce flawed results.

In order to mine the essential principles of peacemaking, we must first bulldoze faulty foundations. We must strip away false ideas and seek a fresh start. *The Secrets of Peacemaking* does not present newly invented concepts. Instead, it uncovers and reveals the lost or hidden truths of all ages, truths that have been buried for so long they now strike peacemakers as unconventional, even unorthodox.

Secrets takes a far-reaching view, which is to say a spiritual view, of peace. For the purposes of this volume, "peacemaking" is not limited to the sort of conflict resolution used to settle commercial disputes, nor does it refer exclusively to patching up minor squabbles or overcoming communication difficulties. Rather, in this work, "peacemaking" describes inspired efforts to infuse all Creation with a supernatural peace. Some call it world peace. Christians often refer to it as the Peace of Christ.

The *Secrets* approach avoids secular paradigms. Such models fail because they exclude all supernatural aspects of life. In other words, they lack a comprehensive view of reality, which renders them ineffective. When peacemakers exclude the supernatural, the outcomes they achieve are less than satisfying. Peace does not endure.

A word of warning: though the *Secrets* approach produces the greatest rewards, it also requires significantly more work. As aspiring peacemakers unfold and examine each core principle, they must engage in dedicated personal reflection. Such prayerful contemplation demands devotion.

Many students of peacemaking retreat in the face of such challenges. Uncertain of success, especially when they observe man's stubborn propensity for conflict, they give up before their effort has a chance to bear fruit. Students of *Secrets* should not be troubled or lose hope. After they internalize the principles in this work, the rewards will soon become visible.

The concise peacemaking secrets presented are powerful keys that unlock doors to a vibrant ministry. That being said, doors don't fling open of their own accord. Rather, readers must use the keys given to them; they must take the initiative and cross the threshold, accepting the challenges that come with seeking the Peace of Christ.

May you experience a blessed peacemaking journey; may you garner rewards you never before imagined possible. Let us get started.

ONE

THEOLOGY, REASON, IDEALISM

Peacemakers repair, heal and restore broken relationships. In order to succeed, they must first understand the nature of those relationships. They must know what brings people together and what tears them apart—they must grasp "reality" as experienced by the parties. Peacemaking must connect with the real world by honoring the deepest truths known to the disputants. It does not flourish in the realm of fantasy.

Of course, some philosophies provide a more accurate description of reality than others. Peacemakers who lay aside preconceived materialistic notions and undertake a thorough study of the subject find that the most comprehensive view of Creation is found in the philosophy of Christian Idealism.

Christian Idealism acknowledges both natural and supernatural causes. It explains the power of prayers, miracles, and inspired revelation. It clarifies the After Life, the Real Presence, the Transfiguration, and Pentecost. It helps us understand conversion, forgiveness, and healing. It is, furthermore, the only philosophy that describes a reality sufficiently malleable to allow for the radical transformation of souls required for world peace. All other explanations fall short.

Most philosophies describe deterministic realities so rigid as to allow for little change. These schools of thought do not embrace the potential for significant transformation of the human condition and thus are incompatible with world peace. A valid philosophy, on the other hand, embraces the potential for individual souls to experience conversion.

A basic tenet of Christian Idealism states that all phenomena issue from the Mind of God. All Creation exists as "being thought forms" that emanate from God. This basic axiom posits that nothing can exist independent of the Mind of God. In this view, an "objective universe" comprised solely of material conditions—existing outside the Mind of God—cannot exist. It is impossible.

Christian Idealism also argues that Creation's first and primary property is supernatural consciousness. Therefore, all material conditions emerge from an ontological foundation of supernatural consciousness. The Mind of God is the ground of all being.

In direct contrast, philosophical materialism postulates that material conditions are primary. Materialists argue that all consciousness arises from and is contingent on pre-existing material conditions. Specifically, they believe consciousness emerges from neurochemicals and neurons located in the brain. In other words, consciousness is an emergent phenomenon contingent on a material substratum. Take away material conditions and you are left with no awareness, no perception and no thought.

Peacemakers, however, find a deeper truth in Christian Idealism. Upon study and reflection, they come to understand that God gives rise to spiritual or supernatural consciousness, which functions as the Subjective Ground of All Being. All forms and objects emerge from this primal consciousness called the Mind of God.

In this view of reality, all humans, in their essence as immortal souls, emerge from and exist in a living relationship with a loving God. Christian Idealism's core premise—that all conscious beings (souls) exist in subjective relationship with God—is a vital secret of peacemaking. Making peace is possible because mankind enjoys an ontological connection to supernatural consciousness. Peacemakers discover that the core of peacemaking can be found in the art of reconciling immortal souls—mankind—with God the Absolute Subject.

Theology—the discipline that studies the nature of God and the nature of man's relationship with God—sheds further light on this idea. A theology based on Christian Idealism begins with the idea that all souls come into being while in relationship with God. Their existence emerges out of the supernatural. They do not first come to be and then, at a later time, connect with a living God through prayer or worship. Rather, their very existence emerges from the mind of God. Therefore, man's first and most important relationship is with the Divine.

All other relationships are built on top of this foundation. The primary trait of a soul—existing in relationship with God—infuses all human interaction. Since only theology acknowledges the basic truth that human relationships depend on divine relationship, only theology can truly address broken relationships and conflict. Peace studies must therefore focus on the interaction between man's spiritual consciousness and the supernatural consciousness of God. That vital connection is the sweet spot of all reconciliation efforts.

In short, peacemakers begin with the study of man's relationship with God, since dialogue with a living God is the cornerstone of all peacemaking. It follows logically that success in healing broken human relationships requires a deep understanding of divine relationship. Conversely, peacemakers who do not understand man's relationship with God never fully understand the dynamics of human relationships. They cannot create lasting peace.

The differences between materialism and Christian Idealism are profound; the disagreements run deep. Christian Idealism declares: *subjective reality is the only reality that exists.* All objects emerge as thought forms from supernatural consciousness. This assertion upsets people steeped in materialism. It disturbs those who assert that the world of objects is primary and independent of consciousness. In their view, an objective universe *must* exist independent of man and God. It must.

The idea that an objective world exists independent of a Creator is a cornerstone of atheism. Atheists defend this argument vehemently. Yet they fail to thoroughly examine the facts. They assume that "everybody knows" this truth—and thus no deeper reflection is needed. They fall into the trap of blind faith assumptions.

The differences between the two worldviews extend to the concept of prayer. The atheists' materialistic or deterministic viewpoint considers prayer to be wishful thinking or delusion. But from an Idealistic viewpoint, prayer is communication that occurs in the context of divine relationship. Prayer is human consciousness connecting with divine consciousness. It transcends the world of objects to connect to a deeper reality, to the underlying foundation of all "objective" phenomena, to the Ground of All Being. Peacemakers thus consider prayer a valid factor in reconciliation.

Of course, few people have a true understanding of Christian Idealism. For many, even for many people of faith, the materialist argument seems to have merit. We have become accustomed—even programmed—to assume that a stand-alone objective world exists independent of all consciousness. Unfortunately, an incredibly strong bias precludes materialists from engaging in a closer inspection of the "stand-alone objective world" hypothesis. In their view, reality only goes so deep. There is no reason to explore further.

However, when people wrest free from the bondage of materialistic bias, they are shocked to discover that their belief in an "objective world" rests on blind faith. This discovery begins with the following exercise in basic logic:

In a stand-alone objective universe—one that lacks consciousness—observation is not possible. There are no conscious agents who can observe. Thus, a stand-alone objective universe can never be observed or verified. Such a universe must remain forever a mere supposition. This realization dismays those who adhere to the "objective universe" theory. They are shocked to discover that their argument rests more on blind faith than on logic or observation.

Though we can see the failing of materialism—it must rest on blind faith—we encounter confusion when we shift to Idealism. This confusion is primarily due to the problem of multiple observers. When multiple observers view the same object, they can be misled into believing there must be an independent "objective" universe that exists separate from their observation. It is worth taking time to reflect on this idea, with the help of an example.

Tom, Bill, and Juan all perceive a common object: a kitchen table. It is easy to assume the table possesses stand-alone existence. If all three men are able to perceive the table, then it *must* exist independent of their personal observations. The men leave the room. An hour later, Sue, Mary, and Maria enter the room and view the same table. It still exists. It has persistence. Thus, the table must stand alone, on its own, independent of all subjective consciousness. Surprisingly, that is a false assumption.

Multiple observers can perceive in unison. Together they can view common objects. However, this does not mean the objects they view have stand-alone "objective" existence separate from all conscious observers. Rather, those objects emerge from and are grounded in supernatural consciousness. They remain subjective creations no matter how many people view them. One or two or a million people may look at them in concert and yet the objects retain their inherent property as thought forms.

How can this be? We have observers Tom, Bill, Juan, Sue, Mary, and Maria. But we also have the Mind of God as Creator and Observer. This subjective Mind of God holds all creation in existence. All the objects people view are thought forms that have arisen out of the Mind of God. Thus, there is no separate universe of objects that have stand-alone existence independent of all consciousness.

As they proceed, peacemakers who study Christian Idealism uncover another secret: subjective observation is man's only interface with the world; consciousness is his sole portal to reality. All knowledge rests on the subjective observations of conscious beings. Put simply, subjective observation is the only way we know anything. In the absence of conscious agents, no observations take place. Interface with reality becomes impossible.

It follows logically that when Tom, Bill, and Juan view the table, their observations remain subjective. Thus, when multiple observers view a common object, we can say they experience *inter-subjective* agreement. Multiple viewers who share an observation engage in inter-subjectivity.

This inter-subjectivity does not change the inherent nature of the objects observed. Those objects continue to exist as being-thought-forms. They continue to be thought forms that have arisen from the Mind of God. This is the essence of Idealism: the universe is comprised of supernatural thought forms.

To put it another way, multiple individuals may agree on what they observe, but this subjective agreement does not turn a *subjective* universe into a stand-alone *objective* universe. Rather, we live in a subjective universe in which agreement—inter-subjectivity—allows us to share a common subjective reality.

Some critics quip sarcastically that viewing shared thought forms is simply sharing an illusion. There is a modicum of truth to that analysis—except for the fact that the thought forms are hardly an illusion. In this universe, nothing is more real.

An analogy may help. Imagine we are all seated in a theater and together we view a projection of the Mind of God on the screen. Now take this analogy a step further and imagine the projection images fall not onto a screen but into a three-dimensional space, like a virtual reality space. Each "player" is issued a laser they use to interact with the virtual world and signal their presence. While such an analogy is crude, it helps us imagine a space comprised of thought images.

The Idealistic premise that all phenomena issue from the Mind of God may be the most difficult concept in all of philosophy—and the most misunderstood. It is not an easy subject to tackle.

However, the philosophy describes the only comprehensive reality compatible with world peace. Only a universe of inter-subjective agreement is sufficiently malleable to allow humans to transform violent conflict into harmony. Only a reality of this nature can accommodate the radical transformation of souls required for making peace.

In an idealistic universe, we transcend faulty thoughts of determinism and begin the difficult process of transforming and shaping the reality in which we live. We honor the innate dignity of man endowed with free will. In contrast, when peacemakers think of man as a computational bio-robot, sooner or later they turn to solutions that call for control, manipulation, and programming—"remedies" that are hardly conducive to the peaceful resolution of conflict.

In order to succeed in their ministry, faith-based mediators should take the time to reflect in depth on how a basic knowledge of consciousness is vital for their craft and ministry. In the past, the materialistic bias of our culture obscured the subjective or Idealistic nature of the universe. The secret was buried. Now, peacemakers steeped in the tenets of the Christian faith can use these foundational principles to usher in the Peace of Christ.

In our faith-based reconciliation work, Christian Idealism regains its rightful position as the most accurate view of reality and the most effective antidote to war and strife.

REFLECTION

THE WORDS OF BENEDICT XVI

Whoever looks thoroughly at matter will discover that it is being-thought, objectivized thought. So it cannot be the ultimate... All being is ultimately being-thought and can be traced back to mind as the original reality; this is the "idealistic" solution. [2]

*

In other words, faith means deciding for the view that thought and meaning do not just form a chance by-product of being; that, on the contrary, all being is a product of thought and, indeed, in its innermost structure is itself thought. [3]

TWO

PERSONAL PHILOSOPHIES

Reality is subjective. People journey through life with a "road map," a personal philosophy that helps them make sense of the world. This map, or philosophy, is comprised of a series of cogent statements describing the reality that must be navigated and the terrain that sojourners will encounter on life's journey. It may be formal or informal. The map may be used knowingly or it may operate below the person's conscious awareness.

Each party's map colors their perception of events. Parties view through different lenses; therefore, they attribute differing meanings to the same "reality." These conflicting narratives present a peacemaking challenge, as clashing worldviews often cause conflict.

When subjective views diverge, when parties cannot agree on what happened, why it happened, or whether it was important, any hope of a negotiated peace fades quickly. In the end, only settlements that acknowledge the disputants' perceptions and honor their deepest held beliefs endure. Solutions detached from the lived experience fall apart before long.

Humans craft reality maps from personal perspectives; they view the world in varied ways, which makes aligning their intentions difficult. For this reason, peacemakers conduct regular "reality checks" to assess how disputants view the world.

Peacemakers listen closely in order to unravel the narrative tapestry of the conflict. They want to know what was most real or most unreal about the troublesome events that set conflict into motion. This assessment is fluid. Factors that first appear substantial may later turn out to be illusion. And factors that initially seem minor or insubstantial may end up being the most real and the most poignant.

Peacemakers begin the mediation process by asking the disputants: what happened? As the parties share narratives, mediators pinpoint the events or emotions that are most real to each individual. They are constantly searching for moments when the disputants were "watching the same movie."

At the same time, they take note of the times when the parties shared little or no agreement. Slowly, major agreements and disagreements come into focus. Peacemakers begin to discern the route they will take through the disputants' "reality matrix." Along the way, they uncover potential paths to a shared story and develop ways to weave disparate threads into a unified narrative.

A basic axiom emerges: when people view Creation from different perspectives, they are predisposed to experience conflict. In a universe woven from many subjective threads, we can expect altercations. In response, peacemakers must compare and overlay the individual reality maps, endeavoring to chart a common pathway that leads away from hostile territory.

However, mediators or spiritual directors who attempt to guide others through territory they personally have never travelled tend to stumble. In order to help disputants navigate the difficult terrain of thoughts, feelings, and remembered experiences, peacemakers must be firmly grounded in reality. In other words, they must become aware of their own convictions and assumptions. Only then can they discern the underlying motivations of others. Thus, during their preparation for peacemaking ministry, they should develop a comprehensive view of reality—a strong and well-grounded personal philosophy that includes both natural and supernatural aspects.

Peacemakers soon come to a first-hand appreciation of the inter-subjective nature of reality. As they gain experience, they become certain they can guide disputants—those who arrive with divergent worldviews—toward agreement. After all, they minister to souls, not to robots constrained by mechanics, programming, or biological determinism. They work with men and women who are capable of discovering new perspectives after undergoing profound spiritual transformation. Grounded in the philosophy of Christian Idealism, peacemakers build consensus that nurtures hope. Once they understand peacemaking as a subjective endeavor, they focus their energy on increasing the affinity between souls. Their goal becomes restoring harmony between subjective beings (between souls) and rekindling love for God, the Subjective Ground of all Being. Fortunately, the amount of love that people are capable of sharing is not pre-determined or limited. It is infinitely expandable.

As peacemakers increase affinity and help parties tap into divine love, they open doors to new visions of reality. When people care for each other, they are willing to explore new perspectives. The more they love, the better able they are to operate in an inter-subjective reality. With increased affinity comes increased flexibility and creativity. Great potential is unleashed. New worlds emerge. Conflict recedes into the past.

REFLECTION

THE WORDS OF BENEDICT XVI

It is a peace which God Himself will establish in this world which has seen so much blood and tears, as if at least at the end of time, God would show how things could have been and should have been in accordance with His plan.[4]

*

Only my readiness to encounter my neighbor and to show him love makes me sensitive to God as well. Only if I serve my neighbor can my eyes be opened to what God does for me and how much he loves me.[5]

THREE

CULTURE & LOVE

The peacemaker's worldview may be the single most important factor contributing to reconciliation success. Successful peacemakers see the supernatural origin of the universe in the Logos, the Absolute Word. They recognize that man exists in relationship with God. Their worldview counters the dominant culture, which sees man solely as a biological entity to be controlled and manipulated.

Successful peacemakers, anticipating a clash with the culture, chart a course designed to overcome opposition. Those who are naïve might assume they must mount a brilliant rhetorical offensive in order to defeat unworkable worldviews. Some take up apologetics, the rhetorical defense of the faith. That is the wrong approach. Rather than take a defensive position, they should go on the offensive. They should seek to transform worldviews.

Peacemakers help parties shift viewpoints using the principles of divine relationship. Specifically, they turn to another secret of peacemaking: love begets knowledge. Love opens the door so wisdom can enter. Nowhere is this axiom of greater importance than in matters of faith. When we align our intentions with the Will of God, we generate great love, which in turn inspires great insight. First we love God. Then we come to understand God. Knowledge emerges from relationship, not from philosophical argument. What is true of divine relationship also holds true for human relationships as well. First we love our fellow man; only then do we begin to understand him.

This sequence is vital in peacemaking: we increase love in order to increase knowledge. Increased awareness sets the stage for reconciliation. The greater wisdom individuals possess, the more they are capable of correcting and improving their exercise of free will. Heightened awareness allows them to navigate past the traps and barriers of faulty worldviews.

The opposite is also true: conflict impairs reasoning. People embroiled in a dispute lose a portion of their ability to reason. Indeed, there is a strong correlation between damaged relationships and diminished wisdom. Disputants who cannot embrace their opponents struggle to understand their motives. Confused and hesitant, they commit mistakes. Their exercise of free will becomes inhibited. Emotions cloud decision-making. Due to the loss of clarity, parties continue to harm one another. In contrast, parties who love more, those who struggle to overcome their animosity and empathize with others, tend to have a keener insight into life. Thus, one job of peacemakers is to facilitate an increase in knowledge. However, they know that an increase in knowledge or understanding is always preceded by an increase in love. People do not understand those they dislike. Thus, peacemakers must first tear down the walls of anger and distrust if they hope to nurture the wisdom they need to overcome an impasse.

Peacemakers choreograph an uplifting spiral. First, they encourage simple gestures of affection between feuding parties, which brings the sides closer together. Heightened intimacy then encourages deeper understanding. Finally, that knowledge generates even more love and empathy. This choreography gradually moves parties toward harmony. The result highlights a profound secret of peacemaking: people know best that which they love the most.

Peacemakers who grasp the vital role that love plays in increasing knowledge and understanding better appreciate the manner in which divine love shapes worldviews. Love that flows from a relationship with God is an elixir that cleanses all faulty views of reality. Love tears down the barriers that obscure truth. Peacemakers who understand the relationship between love and wisdom guide disputants to the realization that Christian Idealism is the philosophy (the view of reality) most conducive to loving and stable relationships.

REFLECTION

THE WORDS OF BENEDICT XVI

[W]herever an answer is presented as unemotionally objective, as a statement that finally goes beyond the prejudices of the pious and provides purely factual, scientific information, then it has to be said that the speaker has here fallen victim to self-deception.[6]

FOUR

HEALING HUMAN & DIVINE RELATIONSHIPS

Divine relationship is the cornerstone of a soul's existence. Communication—the full range of natural and supernatural exchanges between spiritual beings—breathes life into that relationship. As peacemakers gain experience, they come to appreciate the true nature of communication, especially its more subtle forms. What they thought was mystical turns out to be highly practical.

This overlap of mystical and mundane, spiritual and practical, informs the working definition of faith-based peacemaking: *restoring harmony by reconciling divine relationship, a relationship in which souls and God enjoy mystical union.*

In order to highlight the role supernatural factors play in reconciliation ministry, we introduce a dual-axis model. The vertical axis represents reconciliation with God; the horizontal axis represents reconciliation with one's neighbors. The axes are connected: impaired divine relationship in turn weakens human relationships. Those who cannot love God find it hard to love others. Conversely, when people seek God's love, they feel greater affection toward their fellow man. In a similar manner, people who reconcile with their neighbors draw closer to God.

There is a direct correlation between the two axes: when divine relationship deteriorates, human relationships also suffer and vice versa. Thus, if peacemakers encounter impasse on one axis, they simply shift their attention to the other axis. They work back and forth, healing the parties' relationship with God and strengthening the bonds between "brothers and sisters."

Typically, peacemakers begin the reconciliation process with an assessment that evaluates both axes. This allows them to detect a broad range of factors that precipitate conflict or impasse. The assessment results clarify the nature of the conflict, which increases the probability of a successful reconciliation.

In short, peacemakers who work with the dual-axis model are better able to overcome barriers that generate impasse. Once they become skilled at identifying and removing obstacles, they are ready to clear the path to the Peace of Christ.

REFLECTION

THE WORDS OF BENEDICT XVI

Since God has first loved us (cf. 1 Jn 4:10), love is now no longer a mere "command"; it is the response to the gift of love with which God draws near to us.[7]

*

Love now becomes concern and care for the other. No longer is it self-seeking, a sinking in the intoxication of happiness; instead it seeks the good of the beloved: it becomes renunciation and it is ready, and even willing, for sacrifice.[8]

FIVE

ALIGNING DISORDERED WILL

In a world untethered from the Will of God, the reconciliation journey becomes difficult, if not impossible. Cultural antipathy toward God sabotages peacemaking. Parties who internalize that hostility run aground and suffer impasse.

Those who seek to nullify God end up nullifying their own existence. When they trash divine relationship—which first imbued them with life—they demolish the sacred roots of their existence. All attempts to negate the creative power of God meet with failure.

People who deny the supernatural origin of the universe fight a losing battle—eventually, they crash headlong into the truth. Created reality is stubborn. It cannot be dismissed with the faulty narrative of materialism. Those who slam mindlessly into the bulwarks of created reality end up shattered and broken.

Men who champion atheism and oppose God not only bring hard times on themselves; they also ruin the lives of those around them. In their rage against reality, they exact collateral damage on innocents. They hijack the peace that mankind should have inherited.

The atheists' worldly antipathy toward God clouds the playing field of life. The toxic smoke of their smoldering hostility sears men's eyes, hardens their hearts and diverts them from their homeward pilgrimage. As a result, prodigal souls, their free will twisted and blunted, find that their compasses malfunction. Trapped in an angry and hostile world, these souls scatter in directions they would not otherwise choose. In such a world, one that lacks God's love, the odds of achieving a successful reconciliation plummet.

When peacemakers are called to the scene of conflict, they seek to disperse smoke, repair spiritual compasses and soften hearts. They help disputants Restore Face and recover their damaged self-determinism. Peacemakers study reality maps and offer expert guidance in mapping new routes through difficult terrain. They help parties redirect their free will and intentions so they are no longer opposed to the Will of God.

After parties regain their bearings and realign with the will of God, the frequency and intensity of collisions diminish. Combatants calm their rage and seek a collaborative path. Life becomes easier, more peaceful.

Along the way, disputants discover another secret of peacemaking: peace requires the realignment of their intentions with a common baseline intention—the Will of God. Parties seeking to align their lives with God's will initiate a process we call divine collaboration, the only form of mediation that allows people to reconcile with their opponent *and* satisfy their deepest personal needs. Peacemakers facilitate this collaborative process of realignment, which is so vital to healing relationships.

In a universe built on the give-and-take of relationship, mutual satisfaction becomes a primary peacemaking goal. Peace can be found only when the needs of both parties are met. When souls exercise free will in an unimpaired and uncompromised manner, they naturally seek the harmony that comes from pleasing one another. Once souls escape the traps of the Fallen World, they automatically seek the joy that comes from repairing relationships and aligning their intentions with the Will of God.

Still, many wonder: is it possible to know God's will, let alone carry out His wishes? That goal might seem too lofty, if it were not for one key factor: man is endowed with the image and likeness of God. The inner nature of man echoes Divine Will. His core essence draws him into divine relationship. When humans are in relationship with God, the mystical medium of reciprocal love infuses human will with Divine Will. This reciprocity of love begins with God extending love to mankind. Man receives God's love and then returns that love in an act of free will.

This supernatural dialogue, the give-and-take of divine love, the fundamental dynamic of Creation, infuses and supports all life. God's love, being limitless, never recedes entirely out of man's reach. It can never be exhausted. Throughout all eternity, man has access to divine love.

However, mankind's ability and willingness to receive and return divine love ebbs and flows. Individuals do not remain constant in their openness to divine love. The degree to which they engage in the sacred dialogue of love is determined by their state of spiritual formation. A well-formed soul experiences bountiful exchanges. In contrast, when a soul's spiritual condition is poor, sacred dialogue shuts down.

This ebb and flow of divine love—one of the secret ingredients of peacemaking—appears in reconciliation as the principle of reciprocity. This principle calls on parties to satisfy the interests of others at the same time they satisfy their own interests. In a reciprocal exchange, each party delivers and receives value. The exchange that takes place in mediation or reconciliation echoes divine love extended and returned. Thus, the Golden Rule becomes an integral component of divine collaboration.

The dynamics of divine relationship can be brought to bear on efforts to reconcile human relationships. This peacemaking secret has been buried for ages, hidden behind dark clouds of confusion that obscure the truth about mankind's relationship with God. Now that we recognize we are reconciling relationships on two axes (on the vertical axis with God and on the horizontal axis with our fellow man) progress toward peace becomes steady.

REFLECTION

THE WORDS OF BENEDICT XVI

For man is the more himself the more he is with "the other." He only comes to himself by moving away from himself. Only through "the other" and through "being" with "the other" does he come to himself.[9]

*

If I have no contact whatsoever with God in my life, then I cannot see in the other anything more than the other, and I am incapable of seeing in him the image of God.[10]

*

Man is a relational being. And if his most fundamental relationship is disturbed — his relationship with God — then nothing else can be truly in order.[11]

SIX

TRANSFORMING FALSE SELF

Our true self—divine self—possesses a unique property. Divine self exists only in relationship with God. As divine relationship diminishes, so does divine self. In other words, the true self does not exist in isolation, as an independent entity. It is one component of the I-and-Thou relationship.

The idea that we exist as a function or component of relationship has been buried for so long that it now seems counter-intuitive. It contradicts our belief in unfettered individualism. Yet practical observation confirms the principle. Peacemaking success depends on uniting that which has become divided; it is contingent on renewing the inherent unity of souls with God. Peacemakers cannot afford to overlook the power of the I-and-Thou relationship.

When people reflect on their true nature—as a soul endowed with the image and likeness of God—they better understand how their existence depends on divine relationship. Paradoxically, knowing God becomes the path to knowing ourselves. Those who do not know God cannot know human nature. They become mired in mystery regarding the core existential question: *who am I?*

Academic study alone cannot answer that key question. Spiritual eyes are needed to peer past the surface and gaze on man's essence. To the uninitiated, unaccustomed to viewing with supernatural vision, the true self appears to be no self at all. As far as they are concerned, divine self is invisible and thus non-existent. They see only variations of worldly identities, a litany of false selves. The reality of an immortal soul endowed with the image and likeness of God escapes their awareness.

Lack of spiritual vision hampers reconciliation. Blind souls become entangled in conflict with other blind souls. They "fight in the dark." Their exercise of free will has been hijacked. A basic secret of peacemaking emerges: all conflict is the result of two or more false selves becoming entangled in hostile opposition.

Peacemakers learn a critical lesson through hands-on experience: people who cling to false-self identities may display a veneer of social warmth, but they secretly harbor evil intentions. Typically, they express this hostility covertly. On the outside, all is well. But on the inside, hostility rages.

The covert nature of the evil intentions makes it difficult to predict inevitable eruptions of hostility. The false self proves volatile. That's because a false self is actually a complex cluster of identities and traits. Any one of these many identities may be triggered into committing harmful acts.

Identities that comprise the false-self cluster do not act in concert; they do not express a common intention. Rather, they resemble a cast of players from a multiple personality disorder. They cause inner turmoil. Their hosts feel splintered. They are torn from one intention to another.

Once people fall under the control of the clustered false-self traits, they become highly unpredictable. They act out destructive dramas and may even experience a feeling of being possessed. They sense that their free will has been sabotaged. Other influences are in control.

The raging false-self drama defies peacemakers' attempts to foster coherent intentions. In order to reestablish control, peacemakers must help disputants jettison false identities. But first, they must defuse the hostility behind the masks. Once inner rage and fear subside, the false self can be more easily stripped away.

This difficult work—guiding parties out of the tangled forest of false-self identities—can be aided by a peacemaker's grasp of the difference between empathy and sympathy. Sympathy resembles glue, fastening the peacemaker to a party's False Self. Empathy, in contrast, works as a solvent, dissolving sticky connections between the parties.

A sympathetic peacemaker will become hopelessly trapped in the quicksand of the party's False Self. Empathy, in contrast, allows the peacemaker to step back and view the situation "as it is," without becoming mired down.

Empathy supplies distance and perspective from which a reconciler can view the conflict safely, without becoming ensnared. It imbues peacemakers with spiritual vision that cuts through worldly fog and thus aids the transformative work of extracting parties from the False Self.

Once souls discover and recapture their true nature as Divine Self endowed with the image of God, the noisy circus leaves town. When their inherent endowment of divine nature is uncovered, their relationship with God is restored. This opens the door to another peacemaking secret: we exist in the mind of God. In order to understand our true essence, we must first acquire a deep understanding of divine relationship.

Mystics and saints—those who have engaged in contemplative prayer, such as Francis of Assisi, Bonaventure, or John of the Cross—conducted in-depth studies of divine relationship. Their lives provide a glimpse into the revealed wisdom that emerges from divine relationship.

Such mystics extol the value of contemplative prayer as a path to mystical knowledge. In most instances, such wisdom is restored only after the person glimpses their immortal nature. In some instances, the nature of Divine Self may be revealed quite dramatically when a soul separates from the flesh body and glimpses the promise of post-mortem continuity of consciousness. In that moment of inspired mystical revelation, the promise of immortality—the core belief of faith—becomes real. Only then does a pilgrim realize that spiritual satisfaction is the greatest personal satisfaction possible. Direct knowledge of one's true nature as Divine Self, an immortal soul, brings tranquility.

Peacemakers trained in the secrets of peacemaking thus encourage parties to view solutions to conflict in a transcendent context. They also foster divine collaboration, a search for mutual satisfaction that acknowledges the participants' immortality.

REFLECTION

THE WORDS OF BENEDICT XVI

Sin is loss of relationship, a disturbance of relationship, and, therefore, it is not restricted to the individual.[12]

*

If, then, the essential characteristic of man is his likeness to God, his capacity for love, then humanity as a whole and each of us individually can only survive where there is love and where we are taught the way to this love.[13]

*

Only being loved is being saved, and only God's love can purify damaged human love and radically re-establish the network of relationships that have suffered from alienation.[14]

SEVEN

EVIL & THE SPIRITUAL WARRIOR

Destructive hidden influences cause much of the conflict that mars our world. These covert agents sabotage reconciliation by engaging in whispering campaigns, spreading gossip and undermining relationships. They traffic in character assassination. Employing deception, they fuel opposition to the Will of God and create distrust that destroys loving relationships. Such hidden influences actively block the path to peace. Working in the shadows, they remain undetected.

Parties who have fallen under the spell of destructive hidden influences arrive at mediation distraught, suffering fear and distrust. Although their unsettled state of mind has been engineered by covert destructive influences, they may believe their visible adversary, seated across the table, is the sole cause of their distress.

Peacemakers must carefully assess the situation for the presence of such invisible influences. They must become detectives skilled at exposing disguised villains. Their conflict assessments, designed to detect *destructive hidden influences*, are a vital tool in the effort to reconcile a fallen world. Successful reconciliation depends on the sleuthing skills of peacemakers.

If these destructive influences remain active but hidden, they can do incredible damage. They infect people with evil intentions that prove to be highly contagious. Initially, their victims may battle the negative impulses, but eventually they become overwhelmed and lose control of their free will. Subsequently, the covert influences trigger victims' fears, which sends them into hiding. Haunted by fear, these victims abandon their true nature and don disguises (or false-self masks). This is the pattern of events that befall souls trapped in the deceptive web woven by destructive hidden influences. Peacemakers who understand this dynamic are better able to help parties recover their peace and self-determinism.

Disputants who don't have access to faith-based reconciliation experience a downward spiral. The fear becomes debilitating; it grows so intense that trapped souls become overwhelmed with a compulsion to battle all perceived threats. They strike out at the smallest provocation. The slightest insult triggers their hostile response. Unrelenting fear drives their desire to destroy the source of any threat—real or imagined. As their perception of threat escalates, they become increasingly suspicious and hostile toward their fellow man. Conflict consumes their lives. The world looks dark and dangerous. As a result of hidden destructive influences stoking their fears, they feel under siege.

The fear they suffer comes in a variety of forms. Fear may be situational. For example, a person may fear losing their job or their status. They fend off the potential threat by covertly undermining co-workers and bosses. They become a destructive hidden influence spreading gossip or rumor. In most instances, the threat is not based in reality. Rather, the office gossip or other destructive influence uses rumor to seed the initial fear.

A second type of fear arises from unhealed physical, emotional, mental, or spiritual wounds. When a person dreads being hurt again, they constantly fight yesterday's battles. The enemies they fight in the present are proxy enemies—substitute opponents that remind them of offenders out of the past—opponents who are usually long gone. Typically, people "recruited" into the role of proxy enemies are confused by the conflict—they have no idea why the other person picked a fight. They do not realize they are merely "stand-in" opponents, not the real enemy.

The whispers of a destructive hidden influence trigger fear; the person with unhealed wounds worries they will be hurt again. Typically, the whispers are nothing more than generalities that paint a picture of an unsafe environment. Danger lurks in the shadows. The destructive influence summons old suspicions, leaving the person on edge.

The most extreme type of fear is existential fear: A person imagines his entire existence is threatened with extinction. In his mind, he must fight off endless waves of potential assassins merely to survive. The person suffering existential fear exists in a constant state of war—a series of battles they must fight with covert means. In their view, danger lurks everywhere.

An especially brutal version of existential fear arises when a person fears a powerful Deity. A person who fears God must strike out against God—and all Creation. Their fear response is intense and destructive. It gives rise to a passionate impulse to destroy—to nihilism. This nihilistic impulse is the source of all evil intentions.

A basic truth emerges: harmful actions that we label "evil" have their genesis in existential fear. This existential fear, which destroys all relationships, is a peacemaker's greatest challenge. It gives rise to a major conundrum: souls who suffer from existential fear view love as a Trojan horse. In their mind, love is a strategy used by enemies who seek to draw close in order to inflict harm. This paranoid mindset—in which even love is feared—creates a special kind of hell. Pervasive fear drives a person to commit harmful acts. Those misdeeds are justified as defenses against perceived threats. Conflict escalates.

Only one peacemaking approach secures release from this diabolical trap: restoring divine relationship. Mystical union with Christ diminishes fear, dissolves evil intentions, and fosters harmony. Mystical unity—"co-being-in-love"—becomes the ultimate healing elixir. After damaged divine relationship is mended and restored, Christ becomes the Way to peace.

But, you might ask, how does this sacred elixir work? First, we must realize that Christ pervades the fallen world with his mystical presence, which has the power to transform evil intentions. Christ does not resist evil with brute force. Rather, he transforms and realigns intentions that counter Divine

Love. His holy presence alters man's exercise of free will, and brings intentions into line with Divine Will. He teaches us to summon his presence so that we, too, might realign harmful intentions—our own and those of our opponent. The transformation of free will borders on the miraculous. Enemies transformed are no longer enemies. Christ's mystical presence alters the very nature of man's interface with reality. Life changes. Such a miracle would be impossible—if Creation had not issued from the Mind of God.

In essence, Christ rescues souls with the elixir of unconditional Divine Love, which dissolves False Self to reveal Divine Self. Evil intentions, those that have arisen out of existential fear to oppose the Will of God, disintegrate and vaporize. Christ's ministry—from Incarnation to Transfiguration and from Crucifixion to Real Presence—engages, battles, and defeats evil. Christ defeats evil by altering reality, using the transformative power of Divine Love. One might call it the alchemy of love.

Peacemakers who seek to hasten the arrival of world peace can benefit from Christ's example. They can learn to wield the spiritually transformative weapon of Divine Love to overcome malicious and destructive agents opposed to the Will of God. With this spiritual weapon in hand, they are ready to venture forth onto the battlefield to minister to parties in conflict.

Once peacemakers arrive on the battlefield, they are drawn into the struggle. They feel empathy for the trapped and wounded souls they encounter—souls struggling to escape force fields of evil intention; souls besieged by destructive hidden influences that fuel fear and incite suspicion; souls hopelessly restrained in the quicksand of worldly desire; and souls in bondage that have fallen unconscious.

Nonetheless, peacemakers discover that mankind, though bound and drowsy, still longs for divine forgiveness and salvation. In spite of their despair and suffering, their hunger for the Peace of Christ smolders like an eternal ember.

As they minister on the battlefield, peacemakers discover that wounded people have also wounded others and committed transgressions when they became enveloped in the fog of ignorance, which crippled their free will. Trapped in the darkness, they reacted blindly, striking out and harming others. Peacemakers soon realize that most people "know not what they do."

As peacemakers minister to drowsy souls, dispelling darkness and layer after layer of False Self identities, they discover a powerful spiritual weapon—forgiveness. They find that people who unburden transgressions not only seek forgiveness, but also become more willing to forgive others. Mutual forgiveness reverses the deadly spirals of retribution and signals a major turning point. In the hands of skilled peacemakers, the scythe of forgiveness cuts through thick jungles of misdeeds and carves a path that leads to tranquility.

Peacemakers, in the role of spiritual warriors, strip the masks off hostile actors. They render the clusters of false-self traits powerless. They transform disputants. In this process, the exchange of mutual forgiveness accelerates the transformative journey from False Self to Divine Self. Forgiveness, extended and received, hastens an I-Thou encounter.

Thus, spiritual warriors transform evil—opposition to the Will of God—by modifying disputants' exercise of free will. They bring individual souls into alignment with the

Will of God, which leads, eventually, to mystical unity. They achieve lasting victory by altering the reality in which conflict takes root.

The power of spiritual transformation, completely overlooked in secular peace studies, has long been a buried secret of peacemaking. Secular paradigms tout "peak experience" or "self-actualization"—but they are not comparable. Spiritual transformation, the actual conversion of evil, only takes place in the comprehensive reality captured by Christian Idealism. Mankind's hope for enduring world peace ultimately depends on such conversion.

As noted earlier, profound spiritual transformation is possible only because divine relationship is the foundation of man's entire existence. When divine relationship is damaged, only spiritual transformation brings about repair and reconciliation. After disputants experience conversion—when they repair divine relationship—they are no longer the same people who first walked through the door. This takes us back to a basic axiom: reconciling divine relationship restores human relationships.

During this intense work, peacemakers stumble upon a major paradox: when people free others, they secure their own freedom. We can state this as a basic axiom: in order to free ourselves, we must free others. This truth may seem counter-intuitive, but peacemakers should know it by heart.

In summary, it takes peacemakers—spiritual warriors wielding truths of divine relationship—to free mankind from bondage. Their victory alone allows peace to reign in this world. Only when people return to their origins as immortal souls for an infusion of Divine Love does peace settle like the dewfall over their lives.

But what about morality? Inspired by our reconciliation model, we can argue that morality flows from divine relationship and comes to the foreground most noticeably during divine collaboration. For our purposes, morality may be defined as "reason that enhances divine relationship." Moral reasoning also guides our reconciliation efforts with our fellow man.

During the negotiation phase of mediation, morality becomes a standard for evaluating outcomes. Moral discernment shapes party decisions and guides individuals as they align their free will with the baseline Will of God. It also allows peacemakers to detect destructive hidden influences that oppose sound judgment, creating dissonance and stirring conflict. When harmony is lost, we sense that things are not lining up properly, but only moral reasoning can help us pinpoint the underlying causes.

Moral reasoning helps us assess our free will and intentions so we can discern when they have become diverted or twisted. As a result, we come to recognize the convoluted output of clusters of false-self traits and begin to realize that these falsehoods clash with the aesthetic beauty of morality.

When we engage in moral reasoning, we evaluate our relationships. Do they seem to be in harmony, creating sweet music? Or do our relationships raise a cacophony of discordant sounds? Only when we think through our situation in the light of eternal moral truths can we accurately diagnose the problem. In short, moral reasoning is a tool that helps us tune our spiritual instruments, without which it becomes impossible to sustain love and friendship.

REFLECTION

THE WORDS OF BENEDICT XVI

The essence of heaven is oneness with God's will, the oneness of will and truth. Earth becomes "heaven" when and insofar as God's will is done there; and it is merely "earth," the opposite of heaven, when and insofar as it withdraws from the will of God.[15]

*

The love of the Son proves to be stronger than death because it unites man with God's love, which is God's very being. Thus, in the Resurrection of Christ, it is not just the destiny of an individual that is called to mind. He is now perpetually present, because he lives, and he gathers us up, so that we may live: "Because I live, you will live also" (Jn 14:19).[16]

EIGHT

MYSTICAL UNION & SPIRITUAL HEALING

All souls are endowed with the image and likeness of God. Thus, all souls possess an innate ability to access the Mind of God. This sacred potential is rekindled during the Blessed Sacrament, when the spiritual consciousness of worshippers co-mingles with the Mind of God in the form of the Real Presence.

Thus, during Eucharistic worship, divine consciousness pervades the corporeal dimension with the Real Presence, which infuses each worshipper with supernatural grace. This sacred endowment of grace cannot be constrained by the worldly realm, but rather rises up into Communion with the Mind of God. That which is sacred in each individual is lifted up during worship. This holy encounter with the Real Presence provides worshippers with a fleeting glimpse of their true nature as Divine Self.

During the brief mystical union achieved during worship, man's subjective consciousness enters the space of Absolute Subjective Being. In this space, the Holy Spirit infuses human consciousness with sacred inspiration. Human consciousness and divine consciousness comingle. Man and God are reconciled.

Sojourners seeking mystical awareness might ask: how is such comingling possible? The answer comes when they realize that they co-exist in a subjective universe created by the Mind of God. In other words, all immortal souls came into existence in a state of co-being with God. Divine relationship is the foundation of every soul's existence.

Thus, an ability to enter into mystical dialogue with God is an endowed property of all souls. The conditions necessary for mystical union are built into Creation. The comingling of individual spiritual consciousness with divine consciousness is a feature of the divine plan.

Peacemaking merges with salvation ministry when it recognizes the inherent potential for mystical union—for Holy Communion. Peacemakers simultaneously facilitate worldly peace and assist souls in their quest for freedom from worldly bondage.

When reconcilers go forth onto the battlefield, they find souls bound by false-self traits fighting in the dark. In their earthly struggle, while hidden behind the mask of a False Self, such souls lose sight of the goal of salvation. They no longer seek to restore their true nature as Divine Self; they no longer recognize their essence as immortal souls. In bondage, they struggle merely to survive. Peacemakers minister to these trapped souls by helping them untie the knots they cannot untie on their own. This begins with resolving conflict and bringing about reconciliation with their fellow man. The ministry then takes on the task of reconciling the soul with God.

Thus, peacemaking ministry addresses both eternal peace, the peace of the hereafter, and worldly peace. In the reconciliation process, the worldly realm and the heavenly realm comingle. We see this most clearly during the Mass, specifically during Eucharistic worship.

When souls comingle with the Real Presence during worship, profound spiritual healing takes place, which hastens the reconciliation of broken relationships. Paradoxically, at the same time souls are healed, they are called to become healers. This dynamic—the healed-becoming-healers—is consistent with the principle of reciprocity. And it is consistent with the ebb and flow of divine love. Souls healed by virtue of restored relationship with Christ are inspired to heal others. They become infused with a heightened acumen for peacemaking. They radiate with a tranquil presence.

Faith-based reconcilers encourage parties to augment mediation with worship designed to bring about mystical union. Nothing ushers in peace as surely as an infusion of divine love received through mystical union. Peacemaking that encourages Communion with the Real Presence simultaneously reconciles worldly and supernatural relationships.

Thus, we come upon what may be the ultimate secret of peacemaking: man in his deepest essence, as an immortal soul, possesses the innate potential to achieve perfect reconciliation through mystical union. In this mystical union, individual consciousness comingles with supernatural consciousness and infuses a person with divine love, the ultimate healing elixir.

REFLECTION

THE WORDS OF BENEDICT XVI

Belonging to God has nothing to do with destruction or non-being: it is rather a way of being. It means emerging from the state of separation, of apparent autonomy, of existing only for oneself and in oneself.[17]

*

The Church is founded upon forgiveness. Peter himself is a personal embodiment of this truth, for he is permitted to be the bearer of the keys after having stumbled, confessed and received the grace of pardon.[18]

*

Forgiveness is, in fact, the restoration of the truth, the renewal of being, and the vanquishment of the lies that lurk in every sin; sin is by nature a departure from the truth of one's own nature and, by consequence, from the truth of the Creator God.[19]

NINE

PEACE IN THE END TIMES

By recognizing the immortality of the soul, peacemakers focus on the disputants' deepest needs. When they can see past appearances to the spiritual essence of the individual, they're better able to facilitate lasting reconciliation. In contrast, mediators limited to a worldly paradigm dismiss the immortal nature of the disputants. By addressing only shallow material needs and acknowledging only carnal interests, they fail to achieve enduring results.

Secular peacemaking, which omits all supernatural concerns, cannot usher in an era of world peace. In contrast, faith-based peacemaking responds to the divine love bestowed on mankind. It facilitates and augments man's innate ability to respond to that love. Faith-based peacemaking restores relationships between humans by first reconciling them to Christ. During such dual-axis reconciliation, people shake off spiritual drowsiness and awaken to revealed truth. Not only do they find peace; they also go forth to heal others.

Peacemakers facilitate an awareness of the deeper spirituality that infuses events. They encourage transcendent solutions, enabling the transformation of evil while simultaneously fostering harmony and restoring loving relationships.

Conflicts resolved with an eye on transcendent factors send forth ripples of hope. Every soul freed from fear's bondage and every soul released from the false self becomes a new force for reconciliation. Faith-based peacemaking becomes contagious — once its secrets are unearthed and applied.

Christ revealed the most deeply buried secret of peacemaking when he promised both peace on earth *and* heavenly salvation. To Christian idealists, the two are inexorably linked. As a result, mediators who diffuse conflict, no matter how mundane, also do their part to facilitate the salvation of souls. In a world crying out for enduring solutions, they, and not the heralds of secular thought, represent the future of peacemaking.

These healers and reconcilers lead the effort to satisfy mankind's longing for love, harmony, and compassion. They free people from bondage to all that is false, all that obscures the true nature of reality and masks the beauty of the immortal soul. In short, they help people realize their true nature, which helps hasten an era of Sabbath Rest.

The link between peacemaking and the salvation of immortal souls is *the* foundational secret of peacemaking. Mediators must acknowledge the divine origins of reality and the immortal essence of human beings if they want to satisfy man's hunger for world peace. Mankind, for too long, has suffered from conflict and war as a result of his spiritual blindness. The secrets of peacemaking dispel the darkness and shine a light on the path to peace.

REFLECTION

THE WORDS OF BENEDICT XVI

At the same time, the devotion of the faithful shows an infallible intuition of how such love is possible; it becomes so as a result of the most intimate union with God, through which the soul is totally pervaded by him — a condition which enables those who have drunk from the fountain of God's love to become in their turn a fountain from which "flow rivers of living water" (Jn 7:38).[20]

*

The living Lord gives himself to me, enters into me, and invites me to surrender myself to him, so that the Apostle's words come true: "It is no longer I who live, but Christ who lives in me" (Gal 2:20). Only thus is the reception of Holy Communion an act that elevates and transforms a man.[21]

TEN

AND THE REST...

Peacemaking requires significant training. Peacemakers must come to the negotiating table equipped with a strong moral compass, a well-formed intellect, and a wide assortment of practical skills.

To start, peacemakers must learn advanced listening and communication skills. They must understand how to facilitate the process of sharing personal narratives, a form of active listening that encourages people to "tell their story." In addition, mediators must know how to frame this story in a way that allows parties to share heartfelt emotions without triggering hostility in others.

Impeccable assessment skills are also required. Peacemakers must be able to identify and bring to light the truth of any situation. By conducting reality checks, they help parties dispel confusion and falsehood, which leads to a more accurate appraisal of their situation.

When it comes to faith-based mediation, detective skills are indispensable. Peacemakers must be able to detect the hidden actors who lurk in the shadows and drive conflict. By "pulling strings," they learn to identify the covert agents who are fomenting hostility. Like the television detective Columbo, they present a naïve face as they skillfully uncover deception and trickery.

In addition to informal sleuthing skills, peacemakers should possess the know-how of negotiators, salesmen and planners. Peacemakers must become adept at facilitating negotiation. Only those who understand the components of a sound agreement can advocate for lasting settlements. As negotiation consultants and advisers, they may also need a passing familiarity with the legal field. Few peacemakers practice law, but all should be acquainted with the basic concerns of the profession.

Faith-based mediators face even greater challenges. They should possess the sensitivity and discretion of confessors, as they often deal with disputants who feel the need to unburden. Pastoral counseling skills help them address and heal old wounds that haunt the parties they serve. They should be able to lead troubled parties through difficult spiritual terrain, which requires a familiarity with the field of spiritual direction.

Peacemakers should prepare for mediation much as a teacher would prepare for class, having mastered not only the relevant subject matter, but also the art of storytelling. A familiarity with history and culture can also help peacemakers make sense of the social milieu in which disputants live and work—the environment that shapes a party's inner narrative as well as their external circumstances. Finally, the most experienced mediators have as keen an insight into human nature as any psychologist, sociologist, or anthropologist.

While peacemakers must be among the most highly trained of all professionals, such practical skills are secondary to a solid knowledge of the core secrets of peacemaking. The essential principles, the secrets of peacemaking outlined in this short work, take precedence over all other forms of training. The skill sets suggested in the preceding paragraphs are valuable only to the extent that they support the fundamentals.

These days, highly trained professionals can be found in the fields of mediation, law and social services; however, few know the underlying secrets of peacemaking. As a result, their ability to secure enduring settlements remains limited. Such secular peacemakers often become frustrated when they fail to engineer solutions that satisfy each party's deepest needs and most crucial interests. In the end, only those peacemakers grounded in the theory and practice of the secrets of peacemaking are capable of laying the foundations for true peace.

REFLECTION

THE WORDS OF BENEDICT XVI

The ultimate root of hatred of human life, of attacks on human life, is the loss of God. Where God disappears, the absolute dignity of human life disappears, as well.[22]

*

Man knows himself only when he learns to understand himself in light of God, and he knows others only when he sees the mystery of God in them.[23]

APPENDIX

CORE PRINCIPLES

PEACEMAKERS UNDERSTAND REALITY

- Peacemakers must adopt an accurate view of reality (i.e. a philosophy) in order to be successful.

- Peacemakers should embrace the potential for change and improvement in the human condition.

- Christian Idealism—the one philosophy that encourages the radical transformation of souls—is the belief system most capable of establishing world peace.

- Christian Idealism, which states that Creation emerges from the Mind of God, is the only philosophy that accurately explains man's relationship with the divine.

PEACEMAKERS MINISTER TO IMMORTAL SOULS

- Successful peacemakers, acknowledging the existence of the immortal soul, encourage parties to view conflict in a transcendent context.
- Man comes to know his true nature as an immortal being only when he begins to understand his relationship with God.
- Peacemakers who dismiss the immortal nature of man and limit themselves to worldly paradigms undermine their chances of success.

PEACEMAKERS SEEK KNOWLEDGE OF GOD

- Humans exist in and for relationship; man can only know himself in light of the Other.
- Divine relationship is the foundation of all relationships.
- Thus, people who do not know God are blocked from recognizing their true nature.
- Individuals who cannot see past appearances to glimpse their spiritual essence find reconciliation difficult.

PEACEMAKERS REPAIR RELATIONSHIPS

- When people reconcile with God, their relationships with fellow humans improve.

- When people reconcile with their neighbors, their relationship with God improves.

PEACEMAKERS MANAGE SUBJECTIVE CONSCIOUSNESS

- Souls, which are naturally endowed with spiritual consciousness, interface with reality through their subjective awareness.
- All knowledge is obtained through subjective consciousness.
- In the absence of consciousness, knowledge does not exist.

PEACEMAKERS FACILITATE MYSTICAL UNION

- Divine relationship is possible because souls are endowed with the image and likeness of God.
- Peacemakers help unite souls with God by fostering mystical dialogue.
- Mystical union with a living God is the cornerstone of peacemaking.

PEACEMAKERS PROMOTE RECIPROCITY

- The principle of reciprocity—souls receive divine love and then return divine love—lays the foundation for world peace.
- Reciprocal exchange of divine love infuses human will with divine will.

PEACEMAKERS HELP PARTIES REALIGN FREE WILL

- Individuals infused with divine love naturally align their exercise of free will with the baseline Will of God.
- Peacemakers help parties find consensus through a process of aligning their intentions with one another.
- Parties create enduring consensus by aligning their individual intentions with the Will of God.
- Mutual alignment of free will with the Will of God brings lasting peace.

PEACEMAKERS NURTURE LOVE THAT BEGETS WISDOM

- Great love brings great knowledge; people know best that which they love the most.
- Increased love begets increased knowledge.
- Parties who find a way to love one another begin to better know one another.
- Mystical unity or "co-being-in-love" is the elixir that heals all damaged relationships.

PEACEMAKERS ENABLE ESCAPE FROM BONDAGE

- Mystical union with Christ diminishes fear, dissolves evil intentions, and fosters harmony.
- Souls naturally seek freedom from ignorance as a way to escape from worldly bondage.

- Dark clusters comprised of false-self traits and identities trigger hostility and drive conflict.

PEACEMAKERS EXPOSE HIDDEN INFLUENCES

- Destructive hidden influences cause nearly all major unresolved conflict.
- Operating in the shadows, such influences trigger fear and foment opposition to divine will, which fans the flames of conflict.
- Christ does not resist evil with brute force but rather transforms opposing intentions with the power of unconditional divine love.
- He pervades the fallen world with his mystical presence, dispeling fear and transforming evil intentions.

PEACEMAKERS ACT AS SPIRITUAL WARRIORS

- Peacemakers, in the role of spiritual warriors, achieve victory by altering reality.
- Peacemakers transform man's distorted exercise of free will and realign intentions that have become opposed to the Will of God.
- Peacemakers untie the knots that keep souls in bondage to worldly fears and desires.
- Souls freed from the False Self tend to become peacemakers.

PEACEMAKERS ACT AS SPIRITUAL WARRIORS

- One secret of peacemaking stands above all the rest: the path to peace and the path to salvation converge.
- Souls that work to hasten the arrival of the Peace of Christ also secure their own salvation.

NOTES

1. Pope Benedict XVI, *Jesus of Nazareth: The Infancy Narratives*, vol. 3.1, trans. Philip J. Whitmore (New York: Image: 2012), 76
2. Joseph Cardinal Ratzinger, *Introduction to Christianity*, rev. Eng. ed. (San Francisco: Ignatius Press, 2004), 156.
3. Ibid., 152.
4. Joseph Ratzinger, *The Theology of History in St. Bonaventure*, trans. Zachary Hayes, O.F.M. (Chicago: Franciscan Herald Press, 1989), 162.
5. Pope Benedict XVI, *Encyclical Letter: God is Love (Deus Caritas Est)* (San Francisco: Ignatius Press, 2006), 46.
6. Ratzinger, *Introduction to Christianity*, 176.
7. Benedict XVI, *Encyclical Letter: God is Love (Deus Caritas Est)*, 8.
8. Ibid., 21.
9. Ratzinger, *Introduction to Christianity*, 214.
10. Benedict XVI, *Encyclical Letter: God is Love (Deus Caritas Est)*, 45.
11. Benedict XVI, *Jesus of Nazareth: The Infancy Narratives*, 44.
12. Joseph Ratzinger, *The Essential Pope Benedict XVI*, ed. John F.

Thornton and Susan B. Varenne (New York: Harper One, 2007), 265.

13. Pope Benedict XVI, "October 31st: What Hell is Like," in *Benedictus: Day by Day with Pope Benedict XVI*, ed. Rev. Peter John Cameron, O.P. (Yonkers: Magnificat / Ignatius Press, 2006), 330.

14. Ratzinger, *The Essential Pope Benedict XVI*, 266.

15. Joseph Ratzinger, *Jesus of Nazareth: From the Baptism in the Jordan to the Transfiguration*, vol. 1.0, trans. Adrian J. Walker, (New York: Doubleday, 2007), 147.

16. Joseph Cardinal Ratzinger, *The Spirit of the Liturgy*, trans. John Saward (San Francisco: Ignatius Press, 2000), 102.

17. Ratzinger, *The Spirit of the Liturgy*, 28.

18. Joseph Cardinal Ratzinger, *Called to Communion: Understanding the Church Today*, trans. Adrian Walker (San Francisco: Ignatius Press, 1996), 64.

19. Benedict XVI, "February 28th: Forgiveness as the Restoration of Truth," in *Benedictus: Day by Day with Pope Benedict XVI*, 73.

20. Benedict XVI, *Encyclical Letter: God is Love (Deus Caritas Est)*, 100.

21. Ratzinger, *The Spirit of the Liturgy*, 88.

22. Ratzinger, *The Essential Pope Benedict XVI*, 390.

23. Ratzinger, *Jesus of Nazareth: From the Baptism in the Jordan to the Transfiguration*, 282.

www.ingramcontent.com/pod-product-compliance
Lightning Source LLC
Chambersburg PA
CBHW060400050426
42449CB00009B/1824